ACCES LIGHT

VIA
THE MUNAY-KI
NINE
RITES OF INITIATION
VIA
THE SCHEMATIC
BLUEPRINT IN YOUR
DNA

& AN EXPLANATION OF THE
COSMIC ENERGETIC FIELD
WE ARE CREATED FROM
AND BORN INTO

BY
LOVELIFELEE

PAGE INDEX AT BACK OF BOOK

POEMS OF MAGICAL WONDER

POEMS MAGICAL IN NATURE

POEMS OF SPLENDOUR

FROM THE MINDS EYE & HEART SPACE

OF LOVE LIFE LEE

SOME OF MY MAGICAL LIFE JOURNEY

EXPERIENCES OF SHAMANIC CEREM

AYAHUASCA CEREMONY'S

PLANT MEDICINE , DREAMS , MEDITATIONS

REMOTE VIEWING , OUT OF BODY JOURNEY'S

AND LIFE EXPERIENCE'S

POEMS AND TRUTHS
OF OUR HOLOGRAPHIC UNIVERSE .

THE PHOTON THE LIGHT PARTICLE
IN WHICH WE EXIST AND RESIDE UNTILL
WE EXPAND WITH LIGHT BRIGHTENING
SHINING BRIGHT IN OUR BODYS OF LIGHT

ILLUMINATED OUR RAINBOW BODY's FREE
ANGELS WE BE IMMORTAL
INTERDIMENSIONAL
LIGHT BEINGS OF CONSCIOUS ENERGY

BY LOVE LIFE LEE

LOVE LIFE LEE
YO RASTA !
LOVE LIFE LEE
LIFE LIFE TO THE FULL
FOR ETERNITY
CHANTING AND DANCING
IS WHAT YOU DO BEST
MEDITATION WITH THE SPIRIT'S
YOU TRULY BLESSED
HEAD FULL OF KNOWLEDGE
HEART OF GOLD
WHEN THE GODS MADE YOU
THEY HAD TO BREAK THE MOULD
COS LETS FACE IT DUDE
AND WE ALL AGREE
THIS WORLD CAN ONLY HANDLE
ONE LOVE LIFE LEE

FRONT COVER

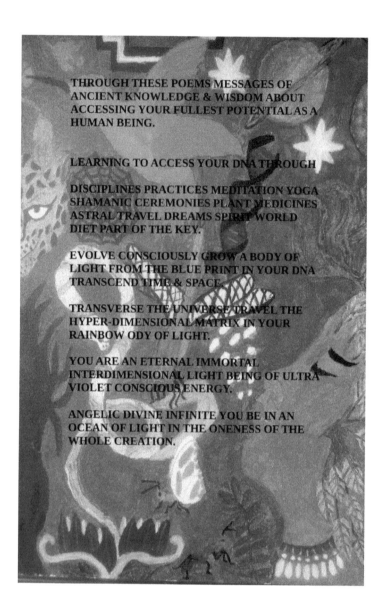

THROUGH THESE POEMS MESSAGES OF
ANCIENT KNOWLEDGE & WISDOM ABOUT
ACCESSING YOUR FULLEST POTENTIAL AS A
HUMAN BEING.

LEARNING TO ACCESS YOUR DNA THROUGH

DISCIPLINES PRACTICES MEDITATION YOGA
SHAMANIC CEREMONIES PLANT MEDICINES
ASTRAL TRAVEL DREAMS SPIRIT WORLD
DIET PART OF THE KEY.

EVOLVE CONSCIOUSLY GROW A BODY OF
LIGHT FROM THE BLUE PRINT IN YOUR DNA
TRANSCEND TIME & SPACE.

TRANSVERSE THE UNIVERSE TRAVEL THE
HYPER-DIMENSIONAL MATRIX IN YOUR
RAINBOW ODY OF LIGHT.

YOU ARE AN ETERNAL IMMORTAL
INTERDIMENSIONAL LIGHT BEING OF ULTRA
VIOLET CONSCIOUS ENERGY.

ANGELIC DIVINE INFINITE YOU BE IN AN
OCEAN OF LIGHT IN THE ONENESS OF THE
WHOLE CREATION.

BACK COVER

4

**THE SCAFFOLDING OF LIFE
THE WONDERFUL WORLD OF
GEOMETRIC MATTER
THE BUILDING BLOCKS
OF ALL BIOLOGICAL LIFE &
OUR UNIVERSE
ACCESS THE BLUE PRINT IN
YOUR DNA
GROW A RAINBOW LIGHT BODY
STOP KARMIC CYCLES & EVOLVE
TRANSCEND TIME & SPACE
ASCENSION YOU WILL ACHIEVE
BY LOVE LIFE LEE**

THE SCAFFOLDING OF LIFE
THE BUILDING BLOCKS OF SACRED GEOMETRY
LEARN THE SECRETS OF OUR PHYSICAL UNIVERSE
AND BIOLOGICAL MAKE UP OF OUR DNA, HOW TO
EVOLVE CONSCIOUSLY TRANSCEND TIME & SPACE
TO LEARN HOW TO TRANSVERSE THE
UNIVERSE WITH THOUGHT MIND BODY & SPIRIT
USING YOUR CONSCIOUS ENERGY
USING YOUR LIFE FORCE
UNDERSTAND YOUR FULL POTENTIAL GROW
A NEW BODY INTO BEING CONSCIOUSLY EVOLVE
AND ASCEND CREATE A RAINBOW BODY OF
LIGHT YOUR DIVINE RIGHT

FRONT COVER

5

WISDOM OF MAGICAL WONDER

WISDOM MAGICAL IN NATURE

WISDOM OF SPLENDOUR

FROM THE MINDS EYE & HEART SPACE

OF LOVE LIFE LEE

THROUGH THIS BOOK MESSAGES OF ANCIENT
KNOWLEDGE AND WISDOM ABOUT ACCESSING
YOUR FULLEST POTENTIAL AS A HUMAN BEING
LEARNING TO ACCESS YOUR DNA THROUGH
DISCIPLINE'S PRACTICE'S MEDITATION YOGA
SHAMANIC CEREMONIES PLANT MEDICINES
AYAHUASCA CEREMONIES ASTAL TRAVEL
DREAMS SPIRIT WORLD DIET PART OF THE KEY
AND EVOLVE CONSCIOUSLY GROW A BODY OF LIGHT
FROM THE BLUE PRINT IN YOUR DNA
TRANSCEND TIME AND SPACE
TRANSVERSE THE UNIVERSE TRAVEL THE
HYPER-DIMENSIONAL MATRIX IN YOUR RAINBOW
BODY OF LIGHT
YOU ARE AN IMMORTAL INTERDIMENSIONAL LIGHT
BEING OF ULTRA VIOLET CONSCIOUSNESS ENERGY
ANGELIC DIVINE INFINITE YOU BE
IN AN OCEAN OF LIGHT IN THE ONENESS OF THE
WHOLE CREATION

Spiritual knowledge of the journey
Within and without gaining the understanding
of the scaffolding of life the building blocks of the magical
world of geometric matter the dodecahedrons & tetrahedrons
and life force energy of our selfs and our universe understand
frequencies light vibration in sacred geometry it's wisdom
connecting to the stars
Connecting to nature
Connecting to Energy fields
An awakening , the shaman and i am
A spirit being
An Immortal Interdimensional Light Being
OF Conscious Energy
Divine we be you and me by Divine Decree
Namaste
Blessings to all that be in the oneness of all the creation

BACK COVER

6

The Illusion of
Rona The Maya of
Demons The ROYAL
Fallen Angel
Bloodlines

& Their Psychological
& Physical War on Humanity
& Information of your light body

BY
LOVELIFELEE

FRONT COVER

MER - KA -BA
(Human)   (Light)   (Body)

...k. This is an explosive, revealing book of ancient knowledge of the blueprint & schematics in your DNA to grow your eternal light body to ascend transcend in the higher dimensional matrix & reclaim ancient knowledge of the fallen angels bloodlines, the five royal Davidic Zionist orders of satanic cult blood sacrifice, their agendas, including Rome's military warfare grade microwave weapons, biological weapon vaccines that will rewrite the code of your DNA, then the elite can parent you to turn your eternal consciousness imprisoned, hijacked, possessed by Jinn & Jinn demonic spirit attachments, the fallen ones...

BACK COVER

FRONT COVER

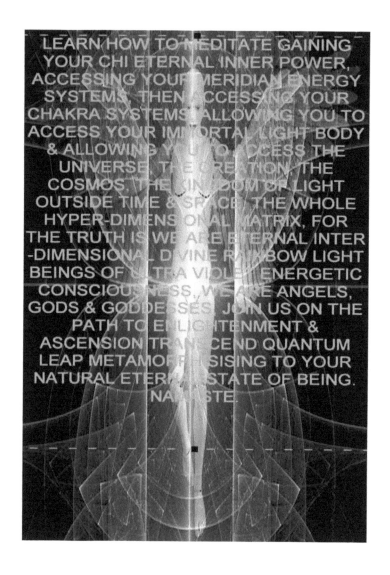

LEARN HOW TO MEDITATE GAINING YOUR CHI ETERNAL INNER POWER, ACCESSING YOUR MERIDIAN ENERGY SYSTEMS, THEN ACCESSING YOUR CHAKRA SYSTEMS, ALLOWING YOU TO ACCESS YOUR IMMORTAL LIGHT BODY & ALLOWING YOU TO ACCESS THE UNIVERSE, THE CREATION, THE COSMOS, THE KINGDOM OF LIGHT OUTSIDE TIME & SPACE, THE WHOLE HYPER-DIMENSIONAL MATRIX, FOR THE TRUTH IS WE ARE ETERNAL INTER-DIMENSIONAL DIVINE RAINBOW LIGHT BEINGS OF ULTRA VIOLET ENERGETIC CONSCIOUSNESS, WE ARE ANGELS, GODS & GODDESSES, JOIN US ON THE PATH TO ENLIGHTENMENT & ASCENSION TRANSCEND QUANTUM LEAP METAMORPHISING TO YOUR NATURAL ETERNAL STATE OF BEING. NAMASTE.

BACK COVER

10

MY PERCEPTION OF MY INDIVIDUAL AND COLLECTIVE CREATION

I WAS BORN IN A THUNDER BURST OF COSMIC DUST IN THE ONENESS OF ALL THAT BE, MANIFESTING IN THE ILLUSIONARY UNIVERSITY OF LIGHT IN ALL ITS DENSITIES AND VIBRATORY FORMS, FOR I THE ETERNAL SINGULAR CELL OF THE WHOLE COSMIC CONSCIOUSNESS COLLECTIVE, BEING CONNECTED TO ALL THAT BE IN THE CREATION, THE BRAHMAN, THE WHOLE, FOR WE ARE ALL ONE in the oneness of all that be in the sea of cosmic light, a swirling of energy, electromagnetism, the weak and strong nuclear forces and gravity, DIVINE ETERNAL IMMORTAL INTER- DIMENSIONAL

11

ANGELIC LIGHT BEINGS OF ULTRA VIOLET ENERGETIC CONSCIOUSNESS, CREATING AN AVATAR A BIOLOGICAL HUMAN FORM BODY FOR EXPERIENCE, TO PAY KARMA, AND MANIFESTING IN FROM THE ETERNAL TO RAISE HUMANITIES COLLECTIVE CONSCIOUSNESS, FOR SPIRIT I BE FOR ENERGY I SEE, ALL AROUND ME MULTI-DIMENSIONALLY THIS IS JUST HOW IT BE YOU SEE, FREQUENCY VIBRATING LIGHT IN WAVE AND POWDERED FORM TO, OPENING PORTHOLEs OUTSIDE TIME AND SPACE FROM WHERE WE COME, HOME IT BE IN THE ETERNAL REALM OF THE KINGDOM OF LIGHT, allowing humans that have ascended opened their eternal light bodies and stopped the cycles of life and death, to evolve to HomoSapien, HomoLuminous, we call upon illuminated beings, on buddha beings, and our ancestors at this time for transformation to evolve to metamorphosis in the rainbow angelic light beings we be in our true nature, we open our light bodies via our DNA within are the schematics of the blue print of your light body and access it will and quantum leap ten thousand years into our becoming, allowing us to be fully embodied on this 4th/5th dimensional earth planet and at the same time we can travel the stars at instant will teleporting to and fro and accessing the eternal kingdom of light realms, blessed i be for magic i see all around me in powdered light illusionary form divine spirit it be gravity, i see eternal transcendental oneness of all that be in creation you see blessings namaste lovelifelee

THE CREATION
THE HYPER-DIMENSIONAL
MATRIXS MAKE UP

So the hyperdimensional matrix of the wole cosmos from the minute and grandest from the macron to the micro particles of creation, the creation has formed geometric beings, of planets, solar systems and spiralling galaxies, from the subatomic to all the multiverses in the hyperdimensional matrix, its all formed from a hyperdimensional matrix of electromagnetic fields of electrical circuitry collective, that is collectively connected, unifed as one and that is energised and manifests all in the creation, the brahman, the whole. This is one created body unifed in a harmonic resonance, our own waters our human blood contains the same divine essence and the molecular alchemy that is the same as that of the elementals, the air and winds, that of the earth and rivers and oceans, our human biological form and skeleton scaffolding, our bones are made up of the same elemental componants as our surrounding environment and that of the ancient plant people and the ancient stone peoples make up.

We are on a continually exchanging light energetic information in a data flow from source intelligence on a continuum, outside time and space to the eternal realms and inside time and space with the body of the universe and with the body of planet gaia mother earth known as Pachamama, and exchanging informational data flow with every living scared geometric biological form of life on the planet, every variation and all the suble differences in all forms of all spectrums of light and of all meaning and expression and vibatory sounds, every subtle distinction and variation of celestrial defusion and maturity within our solar system will and does influence our individual and collective field of divine eternal energetic consciousness.

We now know that circuits of electromagnetic exchange connect us together as one unifed living being in the ocean of conscious electromagnetic light energy, a sea of many seas connected as an ocean of psycho sensory, a co-creative space of time coordinates within the unified field of the cosmos, we are the result of the process of the action of combining and unifing of an amalgamation, so a union of various visible and invisible energy systems that when unifed generates the human biological avatar hologram, the main electrical impulse igniting system that makes available and provides this individual single cell biological unit, the human avatar with the energetic nature of creator intelligence that ignites and gives birth to the field that is the circuitry system. Now in the present time our circuitry system is not running, operating, functioning at its optimal capacity, for now our circuitry system that we are operating on is only running on 60 million base pair chemicals instead of the three billion base pair chemicals that are in the human gene code, so this only allows us to use one fifth of our brain capacity at this time.

Our manifests designs show and point us to realise, that there has been human genetic manipulated modification, by other negative forces and entities that have hindered the development mentally, physically and spiritual of the human species by design.

DARK FORCES ARE AMONGST US

This has been for absolute control and domination of the human race and of our planet, these extraterrestrial invading parasites, that have hindered the human evolution are negative entities and races who are in service to self and not in service of the oneness of creation, they were not here to benefit humanity, they are on a timeline of humanities destruction and to take control of our planet, they are the fallen angel royal bloodlines, the Draco beings from the draco star system and energy entities the archons the jinn, all enemies of humanity. Their intentions are negative of evil intent, they have infiltrated the governing systems of planet earth and all levels of society, forcing us into war and conflict by their design and push millions of sentient human light beings into poverty and disease, to keep humanity in a mortal programming system, to understand the condition of the planet and the human race it is essensial to factor into our calculations, the genetic manipulations of the human DNA for this with our departing from usual orbit of the sun and with disturbances in our mother earths electromagnetic biospheric field, that is creating a fear based degraded paradigm of reality that humanity has been experiencing.

Like all else in the oneness of the creation, the creation of electromagnetic energy information field system, the soul covenant agreement that is embedded in the human matrix, is built on vibatory infrastructure of energy path ways that follow the laws of geometric patterns, creating form and form is the creation of the fabic of consciousness, so conscious commication with sacred geometry is the intrinsic natural essential component of the bulding blocks of life forming the scaffolding of life, the communication with the sacred geometric structure is the intrinsic component of accessing through direct consciousness, and ancient ceremonies and practices as this reactivates allowing us to start the accessing of the divine schematic blueprint in our DNA, allowing us to become our true natural state of an eternal light being, fully embodied on earth but accessing and travelling in the stars in the whole entirety of the cosmos the creation, then we can realise and see the true space time continuum.

The language of sacred geometry is a configurative language of the elemental components of the creative force that gives birth to all life and so it offers a direct condit to foremost principal PRIMARY CONSCIOUSNESS a direct access to SOURCE, this language bypasses the DOGMATIC perimeters of the intellect to transmit knowledge that exists beyond the reach of the programming, the indoctrination and brain washing of religion, philosophy, belief systems or disbelief systems, so sacred geometry is a pure sacred language, it manifests and expresses the interrelating harmony that lies at the heart of creation, transmitting patterns of frequency which resonate with our ORIGINAL HUMAN SCHEMATIC BLUEPRINT.

So the feminine primer infrastructure of all existance, of life is birthed of light formed of geometry, geometric structure of the building blocks of life creating the scaffolding of life in all its avatar forms, so as we communicated with our sacred geometric structure consciously we interact with fields of information, that influence manifestation, their fields of radiance emits a frequency that communicates with vibatory structure of our original blue print within our DNA, it does this searching for a like light frequency with which to resonate, through this resonance feed back the structural integrity of the original human schematic blueprint that is present in the soul covenant agreement is strengthened.

When there is a disconnection of circuitry with the genetic manipulation of the human DNA our heart connection to the creation to source is compromised, and disconnected this creates disease and lose of clarity, a disorientation of mind an altered mental state, with symptoms such as confusion a disrupted attention and you are unable to think with a normal level of clarity delirium, humanity is lost in a deviant zone, relating to worldly as opposed to spiritual affairs, so we search blindly for spiritual reference of source, we search blindly for spiritual understanding and connection, so we can understand self and our surrounding reality and so we can then evolve, metamorphosis, ascend, transcend and quantum leap into our becoming that of a fully awakened and connected eternal light being in our true cosmic divine nature, fully embodied but travelling in our sixy foot wide luminous energy mekaba fields, MER means HUMAN, KA means LIGHT, BA means BODY, so our human light bodies, for eternal light beings we be, divine angels of light, do you see to my eternal light family.

So humanity has been lost in false preordainded predetermined DOGMATIC belief systems that have been tainted by the Draco and invading extraterrestrial half breed royal fallen angel bloodlines to deceive humanity to the truth of the oneness of creation, and humanities connection to the oneness of the cosmos via their schematic blueprint within our DNA, these false narratives that profess to define the origins of existance and of their existance were put in place by the royal fallen angel coven cult. For humanities history has been rewritten with webs that spin false narratives to deceive and control the human race to enslave humanity as mortals, so they the negative fallen bloodlines can have a slave race to manipulate and use, they do this to hide our true eternal identities as cosmic eternal divine ligh being humans, to control us and harness our chi creative energy for energetic parasites they truely be.

This is why we can trust and must connect with spirit and nature and the energetic intelligence that defines the benevolent true heart/mind and nature of creation, the brahman, the whole, there is only one truth, your eternal truth that is dormant in your DNA, a coming together in a flow, so a confluence of cosmic influences rendered this corner of the galaxy a super fertile solar system capable of conceiving innumerable extremely beautiful and delicate and exquisite life forms, each life form a fractal aspects of a holonomic field of symbiotic evolution, each point of light within the field coded, to function as a sensory organ for the development of the integral field, if we were in an electromagnetic resonance within this field we would have of already evolved and metamorphosised into highly advanced eternal light beings with access to all of the hyper-dimensional matrix of the creation and we would be living on a planet of extreme abundance, we would have been in a state of bliss on a path of evolution measured by our ability to translate light, to receive and give the energy frequency of love in all that we create with our divine chi thought energy, this would lead us to function as direct conduits of source consciousness.

The truth is at our present time in the now the concept of progress is sadly measured in terms of material wealth and in the terms of of deadly extremely dangerous technologies that are lethal to biological life forms, there is a conspiring of dark negative forces of the royal fallen angels bloodlines and their allies the draco reptilian beings and energy entities known as the archons the jinn, referred to in ancient texts as demons and devils, these negative forces have no bounds to their escalation of depravity from their forced evil agendas on humanity and that govern our planet and that of our lives.

At this time with the negative forces are geoenvironmental engineering the planets atmosphere and trying to geoengineer the human race by way of damaging and rewriting our two stranded DNA to stop humanity from re connecting all twelve strands of DNA by genetic mutation of our DNA, via our atmosphere, biological chemical vaccines torewrite our RNA that makes your DNA makeup and with the use of military grade microwave weapons systems that oscilated our geometric structure out of its natural state of resonance. The material natural field is decaying acutely at this time, the degeneration of our biosphere ecologically, the collapse of our economic, political and social structures can been seen on all fronts in levels all caused by the systemic corruption, of the disgraced extraterrestrial invading fallen angels royal coven cults intended destruction of humanity, as they battle to take over planet earth for them selfs and to have a small three hundred million mortal human slave race and for them to evolve to immortals.

These negative entities are manifesting and trying to get humanities co-collective consciousness to manifest a far deeper malignancy, where systemic failure is the problem at the core of our fabricated society, so the corruption is systemic in the matrix itself, so we must re-establish the integrity of the true natural divine matrix, by accessing and reactivating the divine eternal immortal human schematic blueprint from within our own DNA. to access our blueprint which is built on the universal laws of resonant harmonics, then we can create synergy with the vibatory infrastructure of our dormant DNA, and then you can access your schematic blueprint of your eternal light body is the transcendent model that offers you the uninterpreted uncensored energetic truth of creation, and of your eternal identity, this is accessed by simply reconnecting to the electromagnetic energy field, and then clarity comes to you of truth that will open you up within at the core of your being allowing you to connect to the energetic spirit energy of creation.

When you have accessed and have an upgrade of energy this revitalises the endocrine system this allows us to be able to receive and translate and utilise the geometries of light, then we can receive and access the luminous density data from the portals of opportunity and evolution, then we can collectively stabalise a new reality of abundance a hew way of existance, a new way of being, then we can create and manifest a new paradigm that resonants with the integrity of the divine source light energetic consciousness.

So we must have a reconnection of the human bio-circuitry through alchemical ceremony, by way of the alchemy of chemistry by way of transmutation of matter of our DNA to attain this we must change our diets and add suppliments such as colloidal silver, gold, platinum, palladium, ruthenium, rhodium, osmium, iridium as these trace minerals tranform our electrical wiring in our human biological avatar bodies from copper wiring to fiber optic wiring allowing us to process a thousand times more information a second, we also have to work at the level of spirit and manifest with our conscious chi energy, for any disease in the body or mind must be healed at the level of spirit, the blueprint in our DNA is a holonomic interactive model of transcendence, a system that if the number of controllable degrees of freedom is equal to the total degrees of freedom, and is the idea that human consciousness is formed by quantum effects in the brain cells which sees the brain as a holograph storage network, so we must consciously by fire ceremony and diet that's key to gaining access and by way of using and linking alchemical ceremony, sonic codes, neurochemistry, sacred geometry and the endocrine system to DNA resurrection and the transformation of the morphogenetic field, this then transcends the degraded mortal paradigm, this will reconnect humanity and our mother earth planet Pachamama to the holistic space time continuum.

In the now our mother earth planet and the human race as well as our solar system are in the process of an accelerated evolutionary state via a raising of energy fields by the returning ascension energy wave from the centre of the milky way, this raises our planetry and our physical vibration and this raises our consciousness, so as these cosmic energies move through the planets in our solar system and the alignments that are bringing the momentum of this age of aquarius, the golden age to its grand finale, its punctuated equilibrium, so what we see as negative and dark energies is the darkness of the womb of creation that then gives birth to new evolved life.

So the more we appreciate and understand in our comprehension of the progressive influences that are driving the present now at this time of transition of change in our evolution, then we can consciously connect and interacte then implicating our selfs and we will benefit from the eternal opportunities of access that are available at this time of culmination, allowing us to evolve ascend, transcend, metamorphosis and quantum leap into our beoming, of our true natural state of eternal embodied light beings back to the true nature of angelic light beings embodied as human beings on planet earth, awesome love it, magical in nature, magical in essence, for divine we be you and me, do you see my eternal light family.

As we today on earth watch the fall, the collapse and destruction, the deteriation within all aspects and levels of our society and world structures we can welcome it knowing it's a time of rebirth, a time of revolution and evolution, so we can rejoice in the collapse of society and in the signs of decay and see it as the time of humanities deliverance from a stale old dualistic paradigm, then we have to accept and embrace our collective responsibility to achieve a higher level of personal transformation, because this will change and impact the human morphogenetic field, and humanities collective morphogenetic field, as we access transformation on that level of the matrix, we then can access sustainable enlightenment on a continuum, and then the conscious evolution on a planetary scale can manifest into being in the creation.

The awakened alchemist of the 21st century knows the ultimate goal is transcendence of duality.

Now we are in a time of of great spiritual awakening, a time of spirituality and new

Perceptions and realizations of synthesis of science, that recognizes matter and spirit to be one energy in different stages of manifestation, that alters the way we perceive our surrounding reality and our selfs. So then essential understanding naturally leads the intrinsic to the theoretical base of this higher physics of creation, it is the recognition of the holographical nature of all creation continuum of manifestations, so when we except and embrace this holonomic awareness we can then on deeper levels appreciate and acknowledge, the symbiotic resonance that actually defines us as single separate individual cells from source of oneness, and as individualised aspects of the one unified body of the divine cosmic ultra violet light energetic consciousness, an ocean of divine transcending light on a continuum.

When you start to perceive the holistic model it stirs and creates a growth, an expanded awareness within and we perceive our physical bodies in a different light, literally and this is inspiring so you want to access your light body and return to your cosmic natural state of eternal being and access and travel in the hyper-dimensional matrix, the prospects and potential are so exciting, to be able to return home, to outside time and space at will in the eternal realms. For when you comprehend that we have already manifested as every race and species of this universe over the last 13.82 billion years like I do, you yearn and need change, evolvtion, transcending, quantum leaping ten thousand years into your becoming, cause the fallen angel royal coven cult that controls earth with their negative draco allies, are on a manifested negative devolved timeline of returned karma of 26-78 thousand years of continuum of life times of suffering, of all that they caused to humanity and many other races, so eternal transcendental in my true nature of a fully embodied light being I shall be, and so it shall be done for I humble say it shall and so it will be, manifested already I see.

So this expanded awareness then influences us to perceive an experience by exploration of the concept of regeneration at the fucrum level, which is the key level of activity in particular pivot point, and we can do this by manifesting a change in our behaviourial patterns and routines, we do this at the core at the level of spirit by affecting the manifestation before it occurs, affecting the core beginings of the manifestation from where it starts from and emerges, so then we must learn with this knowledge to be a master of our inner selfs, a master of our chi light conscious thought energy and spoken word, aware they are creating the sacred geometric matter reality that surrounds us, we then must become master magicians of light energy so we can weave light into the fabric of time and space, while fully embodied at will creating and manifesting abundance for all on earth and for all sentient life from love/light consciousness, we then discover how to interact and to co-create reality unifed united as one, for oneness is all their truly be.

We then start to comprehend our true spiritual nature and identify spiritually to all in creation, we then can come to realise that our human physical sacred geometric avatar form is the pinnacle of the manifestation of our eternal divinity, that is connected to the oneness of creation, for we are truly ever lasting we are unborn we are eternal, we are truthfully ETERNAL IMMORTAL INTERDIMENSIONAL LIGHT BEINGS OF DIVINE ULTRA VIOLET ENERGETIC CONSCIOUSNESS, we are eternal WIZARDS AND WITCHES of LIGHT ENERGY, we are MAGICIANS OF LIGHT weaving our chi energetic conscious thought energy into the fabric of time and space on a continuum, we are awesome. Remember there was never a time we did not exist for we are eternal light energy that metamorphosises on a continuum, so there will never be a time when we shall cease to exist for eternal divine light beings we shall always be, on a continuum of existance on all levels and multitudes of experience. So the human being schematic blueprint is genius it's a master piece design and is the sensory organ for the planetary ascension, so then you can see the planet earth is the sensory organ for human ascension, we then perceive the human biological avatar body as a tool an instrument, so we can have a transcendental experience and transcend this reality of fear, our culture and society as a whole are manifesting, by manipulation of negative forces. We can then through the remanifestation and resurrection then get access to our full genetic material potential, becoming the goddesses and gods we truly be, we then create a new peaceful co-existence paradigm of existance this is spoken of in all ancient texts, as the golden age, the golden age of aquarius.

The human experience in its fully embodied state of eternal oneness consciousness, is an extremely intense experience at times for the power of the mind with channelled eternal ultra violet light energetic consciousness is so sensitive, it can sense and feel all resonance in creation, so the mind is more powerful than any technology with atoms or particals, the mind connected to eternal oneness consciousness is more powerful and faster at processing information and can comprehend beyond any technologies in creation, we are awesome the human biological avatar body is power full, its vocalization of the spoken word, created geometric matter and combined with the eternal chi divine energy manifesting geometric structure into being into life in the creation, with our power of manifesting imagination into creation on a continuum, we can explore any time continuum any space in the creation on an energy level in the universe and access other universal chakras via your heart chakra then travel and explore them also with full access to the eternal immortal realms of creation, its magical in spirit and magical in nature for divine essence it truly be.

Through ancient knowledge from the south American peruvian Laiki people, medicine men and women known as earth keepers of a ancient body of prophecy, but more importantly they are the keepers of a body of processes that can help us evolve and step into who we are becoming ten thousand years from now, by reinforming our DNA to grow are eternal light bodies, we also through other healing arts and healing practices are understanding the the bodies electromagnetic energy fields, and the importance of our bio chemistry and nero biology, and with genetic discovers we have come to the consclusion that our biological chemistry directly effects our consciousness, we can then perceive our DNA has mutated, as we know by genetic manipulation by dark negative entities, the connection is clear with clarity that the resulting destruction of our planet, the terrible state of our society and social structure is a direct result of the genetic manipulation, from DNA that was a twelve stranded to a two stranded DNA, this enslavement by other beings causes all the suffering we see today, this is not from a degenerative of circumstances and are not from the corruption of human nature, but from this deviant programming of our DNA, we see that this occurred at the origins, at the time the manipulated modifications of our human schematic blueprint were altered and ten strands deactivated via genetic manipulation. That is why our surrounding visual matrix reality a duality paradigm is reflected in a fear based degraded state of co-creative collective consciousness at this time, and also with the continuum attack on the narrative of reality pushed on mainstream civilian society, by the digraced negative royal fallen angel bloodlines covens cult.

In our past at the beginning of this 26000 year cycle as waves of energy left our solar system heading for the centre of the milky way, its now returning back from the centre of the milky way and these waves of energy returning are what will raise consciousness and the vibatory resonance to a $4^{th}/5^{th}$ dimensional reality, so the alignment of earth in the solar system in the present is alined with the centre of the galactic core allowing the energy to come fourth allowing us to connect to the heart of the cosmos, these energetic density waves increase and are more rapidly passing through mother earth and through humanity and all inhabitants of the planet.

So these returning ascension energetic waves are activation energetic streams with photonic codes inbeded within them to raise the vibatory density and raises consciousness, as it's a download of source consciousness, that is geometric in in nature, in structure to upgrade the stimulation of higher consciousness, fed into the fabric of the energetic waves of ascension, this changes with the evolution of our symbiotic relationship with light, and with the cosmos as a whole, the relationship we have with our planet Gaia our mother earh know as Pachamama, and with humanity with each other and with evey planet in our solar system and that of the 52 solar systems in our star cluster.

So now in the present is the time to access these subtle cosmic energetic influences, and gain access to these codes of higher consciousness, to do this we have to connect to the higher frequencies of light, become symbiotic with light so we can recalibrate with this cosmic consciousness, we have to use focused awareness to translate, receive and utilise this cosmic vibration of light.

We now understand that humanities circuitry was disconnected when we were genetically farmed thousands of years ago, by the Draco beings from the Draco star system by disconnecting ten out of our twelve strands of DNA, leaving us only connected and operating on two stranded DNA, this is why we have been unable to utilise and decipher the data from the full spectrum of light. Now we know light is an archetypal form of consciousness that is coherent always consistent and logical, this is the supreme organising principle of creation, and that of our sun a conduit that is embodied with the luminous radient cosmic conscious energy, when we understand our connect to planet earth and the body of the sun, we see our co-creative relationship, then our archetypal identity is perceived by our selfs. We come to understand that our sun translates the intelligence of the matrix, of informational codes and emmites these outwards from source energetic consciousness, that has come from the galactic core center that are projected as light energetic waves.

So how do we access and receive this cosmic light, well our human biological avatar body vessels are the conduits as a biological organ of circuitry, able to access this resonance of light frequency, we decode it once recieved and then its transmitted into the morphogenetic field of our mother earth, Pachamama's consciousness, depending on the integrity of the coded frequency and its range we can down load the divine consciousness energy, this dictates are co-creative collective consciousness paradigm reality that we experience, for the human biological avatar body design is an alchemical master piece and was created to facilitate and elucidate the pure essence of divinity light, as our star gates in time and space open divine consciousness flows through portholes, then we can create and conduct a benevolence of our conception a beautiful magical symphony of creation via the master piece instrument of the human avatar, then individually we can express a sentient harmonic fractal of our consciousness.

So our sun is communicating a cascade of radiant matrices by generating a photonic matrix of creation, these radiant matrices are extending outwards towards the planet earth to connect with the resonance field of earth so then matter can be conceived and formed into manifestation, this is called a sacred communion between the father sun consciousness and the mother earth which allows the birth of form, the birth of sacred geometric matter the building blocks of the scaffolding of life in all its wide spectrums of forms of life, from the bipedal to the four legged, the two legged, the creepy crawlers, the finned, the winged, the furred all of our animal fauna relations, and the trees, shrubs, plants, flowers all of the flora, comined unifed the father sun consciousness with mother earths electromagnetic field realises interference patterns of geometries that nest seamlessly birthing and morphing ever more dense fields of manifestation, then cohering into the cyrstalization form of crystalized matter, this allows translation of lights subtle inpulses as life is formed in all its glorious variety of species. So our mother earth transforms the awareness of the father sun consciousness into the oscilating vibatory living poetry of life matter form, that is viberant in all specturms of colour, frequencies of sound that is alive with the conscious sense of feeling.

So the connection of our psyche and our sun is it represents the ultimate comprehensive monadic geometry of existance, father sun is main prime connection to the benevolence of our creation, the suns light consciousness is the counter resonance field for our divine eternal immortal schematic blueprint, for our personal journey of evolving and metamorphosising and our journey of accessing enlightenment is not simply a conceptual acquisition, it is actually a literal ability to become resonant with the evolutionary propensities in the geometries of light, for we do not need mediators between our selfs and the benevolence of our creation, we have stepped beyond the control systems of religion and stepped beyond belief systems from governments and there political parties that have had concealed within them enemies of humanity, that have been leading humanity away from the path of immortality for greed and control of a mortal race to harness and utilize their life force energy.

For right now in the present there is only the truth of source consciousness in the present moment that is being transmitted from the heart of the cosmos, that is pulsing energetic waves through creation and transmitting its message through the divine rays of source light, the sun the sustainer of life that is now projecting the assimilation and translation of light, as information is integral to the process of individual and collective transcendence from this fear based mortal paradigm, it is the integrity of our circuitry that is reliant for our ability to assimilate light, to process the information field and the codes embedded within, and especially the very specifically the endocrine systems it sustains. So therefore the importance of the reconnection of circuitry is fundamental to the transcendence of the death, life, rebirth cycles, and now is the time of the cycle of evolution the time of ascension, transcendence, metamorphosising and quantum leaping into who we are becoming.

So we now know and understand that source consciousness manifests and sustains all life in the cosmic creation, the brahman, the whole, it is the nature of the prime consciousness that is transmitted from the benevolent heart of creation with the female and male tantric potencies of creation, that energetically manifests as magnetism and electricity, the human biological avatar bio-computer is the conduit that the creative source code is down loaded into, via the circuitry which is the delivery system, but because the human DNA was manipulated and genetically turned off by the negative forces of the Draco species and with the psychosocial, chemical and the programming, indoctrination and brainwashing manipulations of humanities consciousness, our main circuits within our bio-system have been disconnected, this disconnection of the human bio-circuitry has by design of the negative forces lead us to be deficient in the supply of electromagnetic life sustaining energy, that has produced humanities extremely limited capacity and capability to activate and express the full spectrums of sources divine eternal immortal blueprint.

Humanities complete deprivation of this most elementary life force energy system has left humanity and reduced us to be conflict driven and to be a regressed mortal race, forcing us to collectively co-create and manifest a fear based paradigm, but now we have the opportunity to have a reconnection of the individual human avatar bio-circuitry this will enable us to establish a full sentient resonant harmonic, allowing us to transmit into the unified field of collective consciousness, then we will come to a point that the critical mass has been reached, achieved then there is a transformation of the morphogenetic field and our awareness will have a realization of this process, then the full spectrum of creations frequencies can broadcast through a multitude of reactivated units of the human circuitry, this will destabilize and overthrow, bring down and subvert corrupt archetypal references this will then fascilitate the redefinition of god in the human psyche, (its funny to me in this moment as a child at fifthteen years old I was already aware of extraterrestrials and was studying them and their interactions with many groups of earths societies, at that point in time I believed god meant genetic ordnance department).

So we now know form follows frequency so the the collective wave form of a newly formed calibrated human race will now see the mortal prison and break through its confines, this will allow us to create a new model and then generate a new paradigm of existance, one of immortality by reflecting the full spectrums of the divine blueprint embedded in the human avatar matrix. This then allows the reconnection of the bio-circuitry this will recalibrate the frequency of the individual and the co-creative collective human race as a unifed field, then relating to the origin to the cosmogenic order of its solar system, allowing us to connect with our true divine eternal identity as an immortal race, we are able to travel and access any energy level and any timelines in the universe, humanity collectively and all of us individually main goal at this time, our no one prime purpose is the reconnection of the human avatar bio-circuitry. So we can ascend, transcend and quantum leap into our becoming, returning home to the eternal realms no longer bound by time and space, for eternal immortal interdimensional light beings we be of ultra violet divine energetic consciousness, Amen blessings to all sentient life in creation, NAMASTE LOVELIFELEE.

THE MUNAY-KI RITES
THE
NINE RITES OF INITIATION

INTRODUCTION

The sacred Munay-Ki rites are the
spiritual initiation rites of the medicine
men, and medicine women the
medicine peoples of the Americas, they
allow access to the schematic blueprint
in your supposed assumed junk DNA to
activate your eternal light body, they
are a nine step process for healing the
wounds from our pasts, in this life time
and other past life times that we have
carried in our luminous energy fields
the software that informs the hardware
the DNA to grow the physical biological
avatar body, and to heal wounds from
our childhood and the wounds of our
linerages of ancestors, and to heal the
genetic inheritance and karmaic
inheritance that we are born into this

life with. Dr Alberto Villoldo is a medical anthropologist who began researching the human mind, how it creates pshosimatic health and disease, when he was younger and early in his training he left his laboratory facility at San Francisco University to go to the American amazon to work with the high medicine people of the rain forests and mountains, later he worked with the last of the Incas, the Inca people the medicine men and women who were known as Laika, the Q'ero shamans of Peru, know as earth keepers who were the keepers of an ancient body of prophecies but more importantly they were the keepers of a body of processes, that could help us individually and humanity as a collective, to not only heal but to step into who we are becoming ten thousand years from today in the now, from the present moment, to allow us to ascend, transcend, metamorphosis and quantum leap into our eternal identities, allowing us to evolve back to an immortal race.

They are the keepers, the earth keepers of a prophecy that talks of the time 2012 as a troubling time of a catacalsmic time for the earth, as a time of the calling of humanity, the time of ascension a harvesting of souls, at the same time they talk about a time of tremendous opportunity for humanity to step into a millennium of gold and a millennium of peace, to be able to transcend to enter once again the eternal realms, these are the prophecies of the Inca of the Hopi Indians and of the Maya, and they all converge on this time in history around 2012, they are the prophecies of 2012, from planet Gaia mother earth Pachamama's EARTH KEEPERS.

Just as important as the prophecies are the processecies, the processecies are the spiritual energetic transmissions that will allow humanity and us individually to step into our future selfs and into who we are becoming, to allow us to quantum leap into an entirely new kind of human that we are calling Homo-Luminous, then we will be fully embodied on a $4^{th}/5^{th}$ dimensional planet earth but able to access and travel in our eternal light bodies, a sixty foot field of light that surrounds the physical biological avater body, we will evolve into immortal beings and an immortal race.

The Q'ero shamans the Lakia people the earth keepers of old recognise that we have a luminous energy field that surrounds and envolopes the physical body and that arranges systematically in order that organizes the body as a magnet does iron filings on top of a

Table top made of a piece of glass, the luminous energy field is the software that informs the DNA which is the hardware. The hardware DNA manufactures the body, so when we download the latest version of the software by reaching into the future and stepping into our future selfs and who we are becoming and receiving the schematic blueprint instructions that will rewrite so reprogramme our DNA, that will help and allow us to create new bodies that age differently, that heal differently and that die differently.

This is the favourable juncture of circumstances the opportunity that we have been waiting for, and that we have today in the now in the present because the Lakia the earth keepers of old understand that evolution does not happen only in between generations like we understand or think of in

Biology terms, they the earth keepers understand that evolution happens within generations, that we are manifesting and creating a new body every eight months, not a single micron cell or molecule in your body remains there any longer than eight months. So that means that who you are in the now today in the present, eight months ago was streams and rivers the lakes and deer and elk and trout and the order of the cetacea the dolphins, whales, porrpoise and condor, eagle, eight months from now you will grow an entirely new body that can be a replica of the one you had eight months ago, that is still informed by your karma by genes that you inherited from the DNA of your parents or you can grow a Luminous Body that will be informed by who you are becoming, by who we are becoming as the new spieces, a new race of immortal eternal light bings, by accessing our schematic blueprint to grow are Merkaba field of light, MER means Human, Ka means Light, Ba means Body, so human light body, so a new species that is appearing on the planet, from before 2012 up to today, because we are the ones we have been waiting for, light sister and brothers, rainbow family may you glow with all the rainbow spectrums of light, rise illuminated, and glow once more in your, true natural state of being, illuminating all in creation, with your beauty, wonder and magic of manifested form from your heart/mind space.

This is what the teachings of the Q'ero shamans the Lakia the Earth Keepers of old tell us, that we can reinform our DNA, that we can grow a new luminous blueprint, what the Lakia people the earth keepers of old tell us is that there's no junk DNA in our biological human avatar system, scientists believe that up to 90% of your DNA is redundant is junk DNA, this is because of their programming and indoctrination, their belief system. We now know that there is no such thing, that that's ridiculous, we know that within our DNA is the pool of information of possible instructions for creating a Luminous Being, and this happening today, this has never been possible before in the history of humanity, it is possible within all of our life times, in the now in the present.

The Lakia are not ordinary shamans they are not ordinary healers and herbalists and midwifes they are the earth keepers of old, the wisdom keepers they came across the bering straits 30,000 years ago, before that they walked over the Himalayas across the frozen bering seas and entered north America 25 to 30 thousand years ago and settled into central Americas and south Americas, they are the spiritual keepers of an ancient body of rites and are sharing them, giving and gifting them and making these rites available to us today, to help us grow the new evolved human being that is emerging on the planet today, who is you and I, that are metamorphosising into eternal embodied human light beings once more immortal ascended, transcended into who we are becoming, that of a Homo-Luminous species, a Homo-Luminous race.

Doctor Alberto Villoldo who received these rites in his 25 year apprentaship with the Lakia the medicine men and medicine women the earth keepers of old, high in the Andes and in the Amazon rain forests, they gave him instructions to carry these rites back into our world into the western world with the admission to never charge for these sacred rites, past tradition is you were bought a gift you would receive a valueable gift from a person receiving the rites, later on as you view the sactions and cautions and precautions, that we should take, you will see that it is acceptable to receive compensation for your coaching and your assistance and your time but these sacred munay-ki rites are always shared freely.

So now on to a pie stone it is a geometric shape known as a Torus or a doughnut and it represents a hyperdimensional gateway that gives access to an invisible realm, that the Lakia the earth keepers have access to as a result of the nine rites of initiation of the munay-ki, the pie stone is a representation of the human luminous energy field, it's the luminous energy field that surrounds and envolopes the human biological avatar body and it is the blueprint for our physical, emotional and spiritual selfs, the luminous energy field enters the body through our feet rises up through the core of the body along our spines and out the very top of our heads and then comes down the width of our out stretched arms, entering the earth for about a foot and rises up through our base at our feet once again, creating a doughnut shape, a torus shape luminous structure that contains, surrounds and envolopes us and permeates and informs us. The pie stones are found through out the Americas, immense quantities of them are in museums around the world, no one knows what they were used for but the Lakia the earth keepers of old know that they are portholes or gateways, but also they know that they are simply stones, that you are the porthole you are the gateway, and that when you become an access point to the hyperdimensional matrix of creation at that point your luminous enery field is unbound by time, your no longer of the manifested effects of only your past of the events that occurred to you when you were twelve years old or six years old, even in a former life time before you were born, your no longer the result of the genes you inherited from your mother and your father, your biological parents, but you are the result of the future of your destiny reaching back like a big, large, giant hand and compelling and propelling you into your becoming, so you are in an affect become a gateway you become a porthole to the hyperdimensional matrix, and after you do that after you go through the nine rites of initiation of the munay-ki, then you can begin to dream the world into being, to dream the world we want our children's children's children to inherit.

The munay-ki nine rites of initiation are a series of nine energetic transmissions that you receive as seeds, they are the spiritual seeds that enter the soil of your luminous energy field, the spiritual seeds are gifted to you by another, that has already received the nine munay-ki rites, and you also, you will be able to give and gift these energetic transmissions of spiritual seeds onto others as well, but only in the form of seeds, seeds that each one of us must grow into great big ears of corn and into great fruit bearing trees, its up to each one of us to grow these seeds, and nurish them with fire, by way of fire ceremonies, pulling the flame into your chakras and filling your entire luminous energy field with the element of fire of flame.

Within the rites there are four fundamental transmissions of the munay-ki, the first one awakens the seerer within you and then you are able to see into the awesome magical invisible world of energy and spirit, the second awakens the healer within you and the healing power of your hands are ignited and this launches you on a process of personal healing, the third aspects are the protections, energetic protections that you weave into the fabric of your luminous enery field. so this then allows you to walk fearlessly on planet Gaia mother earth Pachamama and to walk your path with beauty in the world, the fourth is a connection to a linerage, the munay-ki connects us to a linerage of wisdom keepers, earth keepers from the past and the future of luminous beings that have transcended their states and their state as mortals and have become angelic, this is the linerage that works with you and through you, men and women from the past and the future, that are illuminated, transcended.

The illuminated earth keepers understand the creation of the universe manifests at four different levels, its helpful to think of these four levels as Russian nesting dolls, dolls that nest within each other, informing the levels within, the first of these levels is the level of the body the physical literal level which is enveloped by the level of the mind that informs the body, we know that the mind creates psycosomatic disease and that it can create psycosomatic health, enveloping and informing the mind and the body is the soul level, of soul or of myth, the sacred and enveloping and informing all of these is the level of sacred divine spirit, each of these levels has its own language, the level of the body of manifested formed matter its language is biochemical, molicules and atoms, then the level of the mind, the minds language are words, the level of the soul has the language of images of poetry of fire of drums of dance and music, the level of spirit well its language is energy, pure energy and intention from the source of eternal ultra violet divine energetic consciousness.

The munay-ki the nine initiation rites operate at the level of spirit and utilise the language of energy which informs the soul, then informs our minds and then our belief systems, then informing our biological avatar body and our programmed behaviours and repetitive cycles that no longer service us going forward in life, then when we bring change about at thedeepest level of spirit at the blueprint level of our being, our soul changes, our minds change, our bodies change and the world around us is transformed, a new way of being ensues and becomes our manifested reality, of peace beauty and magical wonder.

At the level of the body, reality is 99% matter and 1% consciousness, at the level of spirit reality is 99% consciousness and 1% matter, the closer at the level of spirit we intervene the more powerful our intervention is, we know we cannot fix an emotional wound by doing superficial things like shopping and buying material things, we also know we cannot solve a problem at the level in which it was created, it has to be resolved at the level above, always at the level of spirit.

The earth keepers understands that there is always a spiritual solution that there is an energetic solution to every problem we face and that when we work and operate from the level of spirit, from the level of the sacred, the level of the divine, from the level of source, we have extraordinary assistance available to us, the munay-ki processecies offers humanity offers us individually the opportunity, the possibilities to take up permanent residence at the domain of spirit, residence in the eternal realms, we remain emanatly effective in the world but are no longer supressed, controlled, owned or possessed by it, we are in the world but not of it.

The Q'ero shamans the medicine men and women the Lakia peoples the earth keepers understands that there are four steps in the awakening of our spirit or our god consciousness, the first is that god is outside of us and that we must plakat and make offerings to this god, the second is that god is within us, the third level is god channels, operates through us and works through us, the fourth level is that god or spirit works as us, that you and I are god mascurading as our selfs, its awesome just love it, for magicians of light we be and while it is easy to comprehend this concept, the munay-ki initiations rites brings this understanding to a cellular level, a visual level were we become aware with concentrated awareness via clarity through breath and stillness and then we know that we know we are spirit, that we are eternal immortal interdimensional light beings of ultra violet divine energetic consciousness, that we are one in the oneness of creation, the brahman, the whole. Manifesting and dreaming the physical world into being via sacred geometric form, via our chi energetic consciousness and we choose to dream a sacred dream, an illuminated spiritual dream. when we function and operate at the level of spirit we have luminous beings available to us, angels, archangels, medicine men and women, buddha beings, Christ beings from the past and the future, ready and willing and able to work with us, to work through us, to work as us to create the new kind of world we want our children's children's children to inherit, to dream a healed and whole world into being, of peace beauty and wonder.

These are the prophercies and processecies of the earth keepers, these are the prophercies of the munay-ki and they begin with creating micro universe in which to conduct sacred ceremony and healing, we create a sacred space, in the western world we think of sacred spaces as places, as churches, synagages, places where people worship, but for the earth keepers the entire world is sacred, and so you learn that you can create a sacred space which is a micro universe, in which ordinary laws of time and space are temporarily suspended, and that you can do that by calling on the four directions, by coming into proper relationship with the four corners of the world, with the south, the west, the north, the east and with heaven and earth, we come into alignment with the four directions of our ordinary world, with the world above us the heavens, with the mother the feminine, the earth below us connects us to the ecosphere to the sphere of nature and the earth keepers understand that when they saluted the four directions of north, south, west, east, that they were saluting at and to the four fundamental principles of creation, the four fundamental forces known to physics gravity, electromagnetism, the strong and weak nuclear forces, every thing in physical creation is made up of these four fundamental forces.

So now biologists have also recognised that the four fundamental principles that constitute all of life, that all of the form and poetry of manifested creation is written with an alphabet that has only four letters in it, these four letters are the four basic pairs of DNA, of an alphabet that contains only four letters and that creates the mosses, the grasses, the condors, hawks, eagles, humans, the oakwood trees and dolphins, whales, and trout, when the earth keepers salute one of the four directions they are engaging with one of the fundamental forces of creation, forces that create and forces that destroy and it gives them the power and ability and the responsiablity to create and to sustain all of life.

The second kind of sacred space we open is an expanding of our luminous energy field, when we call on the four directions we are coming into proper relationship with the four forces of creation and with heaven and earth, this connects us to the ecological sphere, the second sacred space we open is an expanding of our luminous energy field that connects us to the noosphere, that is the distinctly human sphere, it is sacred space this gives luminous beings from the past and the future an opportunity to co-exist side by side with us and intervene on our behalf, this is a sacred space that is opened by reaching up into our 8th chakra, a luminous centre that resides above the physical body but within our luminous energy field, using both our hands together reaching up into our 8th chakra and expanding this radient orb to surround expand and envelope us, in doing so we create a micro universe in which we are outside of ordinary time, the 8th chakra that resides above the head is what in the western world we call the soul, the energetic structure of the soul.

When we expand our luminous energy field we are creating a micro universe outside of ordinary time, we are able to step into infinity, we are able to gain guidance and the wisdom and the power of the linerages of luminous beings, of the angels and archangels the Christ and buddha beings that support us in our work, our awakening and our healing to transcend from mortality to immortality, once more, for we have already manifested and experienced every race and species in this universe after being in the universe for 13.68 billion years, and now in the present we are experiencing the human biological avatar form in all its glory for it is one of the most mystical divine biological technologies of the creation of the oneness of all that be.

The munay-ki is the path of fire, it is the path of lightening, it is the rapid path to enlightenment, it is said you do not need seven hundred life times to experience your true nature as eternal divine spirit, that we can do it within this life time, that we can do it today, that we can do it in the now in the present, we can do it by reinforming the hyperdimensional matrix the luminous energy field, that organises not only our physical bodies but our physical manifest world around us. That is why the core ceremony of the munay-ki is the fire ceremony, because the seeds you receive with each rites are seeds that germinate not with water as ordinary seeds do, these are spiritual seeds that germinate with light, with flame, that germinate with fire, later on you will practice the fire ceremony that allows us to bring the warmth of the fire, the light of the sun into each chakra, the energy centre points in your body, to awaken these seeds that you have received, so you can access your divine schematic blueprint via your DNA and open your light body once more.

The initiation rites of the munay-ki have been released at this time in history because of the extaordinary transformation the planet is going through, use them with caution, use them safely and respectfully, after you receive the the munay-ki rites these initiations are yours to share with others, with loved ones, with friends, with clients, share them carefully, share them respectfully, traditionally these rites were given at the pace that the student was ready to receive them, remember that every person you give them to is your protégé, that you must look out for their safety and well being physical, mental, emotional and spiritual well being, with the intergration of these healing processecies. So that they do not become over whelming for the person you are working with, some people may be ready to receive these rites one per week, others may require one per month, traditionally they were given when the student was ready, some times only gifted once per year, today the accelerating and rapid pace of change has become so great and so extremely accelerated, that we can not wait ten years to go through the great initiations, we have to pass the rites on today.

When working with your students transmittinig the rites, which gives them the opportunity to intergrate at an energetic level, all of the healing they are experiencing the healing of their feminine, their healing of the masculine, the healing of the relationship to the earth, the healing of the relationship to the earth our mother, the healing of the relationship to the ancestors, for all of these healing processes to continue at a quick pace, but at a gentle energetic level with out every popping up into the psychological or bursting fourth into the physical, so that only their benefits, their healing qualities, their rewards come up to the level of the mind and the level of the body, remember that these are transformational processes they are our chemical processes, that we want to maintain at a subtle, gentle energetic level, the way to do this is to continue to bring them to the fire, to the flame, come back to the fire ceremony, if you receive the rites on a weekly basis, hold a weekly fire ceremony, bring into the fire that which you are releasing, take from the light that which is offered to you, bring it back to the fire, the fire is the core ceremony of the munay-ki rites.

The munay-ki are our chemical processes transformational processes that bring about the start of immediate healing at the energetic level, this healing manifests gradually over time at the level of mind, of beliefs and psychology at the level of the body, at the level of the physical, you can make the choice to reside at the level you choose you wish to manifest, do you choose to ascend, transcend and quantum leap ten thousand years into your becoming, returning to the immortal realm, becoming a guardian of all sentient life in all the creation, the brahaman, the whole, in all the multiverses galaxies solar systems, to become a star keeper and a creator, of all eternal sentient life in it magical divine sacred geometric forms and expressions, for angels we truely be.

OUR FOUR BRAINS

The munay-ki manifested and evolved as an energetic methodology to harness the power of the four brains that each one of us has, the human brain has four sub brains within it, the first brain and most primitive is the reptilian brain, the reptilian brain is only interested in survival sustaining life and reproduction, its instincts for survival and sustaining self preservation, then enveloping and encompassing the reptilian brain is the mammalian brain, the limbic brain, when this brain is dormant and its physical functions suspended or slowed down its as if humanity is in a deep sleep, hypnotized, so the limbic brain it operates with four instinctual programs, that neuroscientists know as the four F's, which is fear, feeding, fighting and phornicating.

When we can gain control and start to harness the power of this brain, we are able to step beyond fear, we are able to step beyond scarcity, we start to thrive and live in a world of abundance, we are able to experience intimacy, love connections with others and we are able to step beyond fear, violence, beyond the violence we inflict on others as well as are selfs, the third brain is the neocortex brain that surrounds, envolopes the mammalian and reptilian brains, this is the brain that is awakened when we have the munay-ki wisdom keeper rites, this is the brain of Beethoven of Einstein, the brain of mathamatics, the brain of philosophy.

When the neocortex brain is stirred and awakened through the munay-ki we recognize THE human avatar MIND IS completely and utterly MAD, that we cannot dig our selfs out of a hole with a shovel or spade, we learn we must step beyond mind and into spirit, when this neocortex brain is awakened we step beyond wants and mores and we step into ethics, universal ethics, when this brain is awakened we can have the taste of infinity, access to the eternal, the immortal realms.

So now we come to the fourth brain this is the most recent supplementary enchancing addition to the human neurological apparatus, it is the four brain, the prefrontal lobes of the brain at the forehead, our cousins the Neanderthals did not have this brain, they were actually known as low brows, their brows slanted back, sloped backwards, our brows today slant forwards, we have a new brain structure that they did not have, neuroscientists refer to this as the god brain, it is the brain that allows us to unrestricted and break free of time, to influence occurrences events that have occurred in the past, to nudge destiny of whats written in the stars, your fate to come, the neocortex brain it is the brain of Homo-Luminous, the brain of the illuminated enlightened embodied human eternal light being, who we are becoming, this is the brain that is awakened with the muny-ki nine initiation rites of the earth keepers, your god, you are god as I am god in the oneness of the cosmic light energy ocean, and even through the prefrontal lobes of the god brain appeared in humans one hundred thousand years ago, during an evolutionary quantum leap, in which the brain doubled in size within a period of ten generations, was that the genetic manipulation by positive spiritual entites, to aid us and help humanity evolve at a much faster rapid pace, before humanities DNA was manipulated with ten strands switched off of our twelve stranded DNA, reduced to a two stranded DNA, but change is here in the now the present.

So the human races neocortex brain neurocomputer has not been an activate brain in humans until recently, it is only today we understand and are waking up the potentials and capabilities of the god brain, the neocortex brain and through the rites of the munay-ki, that the earth keepers of old developed technologies for energetically awakening and tapping into extraordinarily vast power of this brain, that allows us to dwell and reside in infinity, free of time unbounded by space, so transcended we become immortal the divine embodiment of creation.

The reptilian brain is a brain of survival, it is a master of survival, it is a master at procreation, we do not need a brain much larger than a size of a lizard to thrive in this world.

The neurological apparatus that we have, gives us the opportunity to step into the who we are becoming into the fullness of our true eternal human nature, to step into our eternal spirit nature, our eternal immortal god nature, to participate consciously in the process of life of the manifestation of creation, of dreaming a new world into being, from the eternal conscious cosmic chi energy of love light, but we can only do that when the capabilities of these neurocomputers have been activated, this is what the munay-ki nine sacred rites of initiation does, this is what the earth keepers of old understood, that when they went through these rites of initiation, they were experiencing and they were tapping into vast and unlimited capabilities of the power of the four brains when unifed and activated working as one unified brain, one unifed field connected to the zero point energy of the cosmos of creation.

MUNAY-KI EXPLINATION

Munay-Ki comes from a Quecha word that means (I love you, be as you are), these are the nine rites of initiation taken to become a person of wisdom and power, who will and has excepted the stewardship for all life all sacred geometric form in the creation. These rites are standard or common in all shamanic traditions, though they are expressed in different ways, practices, forms and styles in different cultures. They originally came from the great initiations from the Hindus valley that were brought to the American lands by the first medicine men and women, who crossed the baring straights from Siberia during the glacial period 30,000 years ago, these old earth keepers were the known as the Laika, earth keepers of old.

The Laika have always been ordinary men and women who have lived extraordinary lives, not born with special gifts from spirit, but have acquired grace, power through prayer, study of ancient wisdom teachings and through discipline.

Some evolved to become chiefs, principals, leaders and healers, shamans and medicine men and women, while others lived quiet lives, growing crops and raising a family. The Laika the earth keepers felt, so knew people would come to the Munay-Ki initiation rites when they felt a calling to do so, as I did myself ten years ago, but received them seven years ago and have practiced munay-ki and fire ceremonies for seven years.

Many of us have had that calling from spirit and long to make a difference to our life and there for a difference in the world, as your manifestations create sacred geometric form into being to create part of this reality, this world.

When you start on the path of the earth keepers with sincere intention and with an open heartand mind, you notice there are many around you, like your self that are awakening slowly to their true eternal identity that of a divine cosmic energy light being and your not alone. You find yourself in the company of other earth keepers that manifested on earth many thousands of years ago, they are luminous beings of light who are now woven in the fabric of time in the hyper-dimensional matrix of life. These earth keepers of old will assist you in transformation with guidance, and combine there power and vision with your power and vision.

As you learn and start to practice the Munay-Ki you will feel the presence and sense the wisdom of these luminous ones, who have stepped out of liner time and dwell in sacred time, outside timelines and space, in infinity, free from rebirth free from karma. The Munay-Ki nine rites clear your luminous energy field of psychic sludge left from life times of trauma. It will raise your bodies vibration levels, these luminous ones are our guides.

These earth keepers come from the past and future, and can help us access who we are evolving to as immortal humans, memories from the past and the visions of the future come as possibilities, because everything in the future is in potential form.

That is why earth keepers from the tribes of the Inca, Hopi Indians, Maya and there are many other nations of old that gather in prayer to envision peace on earth. They track different possible future time lines, to find the time line with fresh clean rivers and fresh clean air with people living in peace in harmony with nature and each other, a time line were we are reconnected to our true nature, peaceful, loving.

The visioning installs it into our collective destiny and makes it more likely to manifest, when we connect and join the earth keepers from the future, we then have available to our selfs knowledge that will upgrade our DNA.

The earth keepers the Laika understand that our genes are not just informed by the past experiences and not just informed by our ancestors DNA, they understand that when you are free of the bounds of time and space, the future, your future self can reach backwards like a huge hand and pull you you forward in to who you are becoming, an awakened luminous light being, vibrating in love and light, moving through the fabric the veil of time and space and infinity.

When you receive the nine Munay-Ki rites your chakras will begin to brighten, to glow with their true original radiance, brightness and you will develop into a rainbow light body, in time with meditation and fire ceremonies to grow the seeds planted in your chakras into fruit bearing trees, you can communicate consciously to your DNA in meditation, visualize and go inside your body and see the changes in your DNA, visualize the cells metamorphosising, see the fire from ceremonies ignite your schematic blueprint information, see your cells your energy points your chakras glowing illuminated, all focused conscious thought chi will help you achieve your desired goal, of manifesting and accessing your merkarba light field.

Then with practice and fire ceremonies the fruit will bear and you can download a new better version of software that informs your luminous energy body, that will then inform the hardware the DNA, with instructions on how to create a new body, that will heal, age and die differently, amazing I love it awesome, happy days, divine magic wonder a marvel of the creation is the human light body.

All you have to do is invite these luminous ones, the earth keepers in when you are ready to to so, ready to receive them, they are our medicine lineage, they evolved from humans to that of angels, some are spirit, some are in bodies but they all have a mandate to protect those who are looking after and protecting and in balance with our mother earth our plant Gaia, Pachamama.

They are the greatest, finest loving spiritual allies one can have, we can access the blue print in our DNA and grow and develop luminous energy fields that of angels in our life time, in the now, the Munay-Ki rites offers us access to energetic keys to allow us to do this, in the now.

As we become earth keepers, we join the ranks of angels from different worlds and were the original souls present after creation, they do not cycle through bodies as humans do, they have ever lasting life and are the keepers of many worlds, galaxies and realms.

There were nine Munay-Ki rites that were given by ancient teachers of old given to them by angelic beings and are now passed on from teacher to student, when the rites are passed on, it is a lineage of luminous beings that transmits itself, that leaps from forehead to forehead. To transfer this energetic information, the earth keeper simply maintains sacred space and embodies the vibration of the level he or she wishes to transmit.

These initiations can not be done on your own, but once you have received them, the rites are yours to transmit to others, there is one sacred rule or there is one caveat, the rites are offered as a gift, free of charge, you may except gifts or donations or you may charge a fee for your time to coach someone as they go through the changes the Munay-Ki brings, but you can not charge for the rites themselves, they are sacred for all in the oneness to access, to evolve.

FOUNDATION RITES

Healer Rite – connects you to a lineage of luminous beings from the past, who come to assist you in your personal transformation.

Awakens the healing power in your hands so that everyone you touch is blessed, there is tremendous spiritual assistance available and these luminous ones work in our sleep to heal the wounds of the past and of our ancestors.

Bands Of Power & Protection – Five luminous belts are woven into your luminous energy field for protection, they act as filters, breaking down any negative energies that come towards the person into one of the five elements, these energies then feed the luminous energy field instead of harming.

Harmony Rites – Transmission of 7 archetypes into the chakras , these are serpent, jaguar, hummingbird, and eagle and the 3 archangels -the keeper of the lower world – the keeper of the middle world and the protector of the upper world, these 3 relate to our unconscious, conscious and higher conscious selves.

Seers Rite - Extra – cerebral path ways of light are installed that connect the visual cortex with the third eye and heart chakra, this awakens the inner seers in you and then have the ability to perceive the invisible world of energy and spirit.

LINEAGE RITES

Day Keeper Rites – You will connect to a linage of master healers from the past, the day keepers are able to call on the ancient altars to heal and bring balance to the world to earth and bring humans into balance and harmony with nature and mother earth, they are the midwives, herbalists and curanderos, this rite starts to heal the your inner feminine, to step beyond fear and practice peace.

Wisdom Keeper Rite – You will connect to a lineage of luminous beings from the past and future, who hold wisdom of the ages from all societies and cultures, this rite allows you to heal your inner masculine, step outside liner time, become enveloped, steeped in the medicine and wisdom teachings and taste infinity.

Earth Keeper Rite – This rite connects you to the archangels they are the guardians of our galaxy, they are the stewards of all life on earth, this rite connects you to the sun, to our local star and to the stars beyond, it allows you to learn the ways of the seer and then allows you to dream the world into being.

RITES OF THE TIME TO COME

Star Keeper Rite – This rite anchors you safely to the time afer the great change occurring, starting around 2012, you connect to your future self and your physical body begins to evolve, the ageing process is slowed and your DNA is re-informed with light and you become more resistant to disease.

Creators Rite – Awakens the creator light within and brings fourth a sense of stewardship for all creation, from the smallest grain of sand to the largest cluster of galaxies in the universe, once attained only through direct transmission from spirit, it is now possible to transmit from one person to another.

As you work with the germination of the seeds in your chakras and put light the element of fire into them you will access the schematics in your blueprint in your DNA and grow a rainbow light body, Joining and returning to the eternal realm, so you must do ceremonies and germinated the seeds of these rites and you will be touched by and be blessed by angels, you only have to open yourself to the wisdom of the wise luminous ones, the earth keepers of old and all will be bestowed upon you.

THE GREAT PRINCIPLES

Non – violence --- Bring no harm to yourself or others.

Truthfulness – Be true to your word and let your word be true, if you speak enough, what you say comes true.

Integrity – Do not steal, not even a glance, walk your talk.

Moderation – Use the life force within you wisely, don't waste energy.

Generosity – Give more than you take, for nothing in this world really belongs to you.

I hope this knowledge plants a seed with you and you start your Munay-Ki journey blessings love life lee.

All I wish for is to see my fellow light being sisters and brothers to have enlightenment, to open there rainbow bodies of light, to stop the cycles of life and death, to ascend, to evolve to Homo- Luminus, to quantum leap ten thousand years into the future, into who you are becoming, who you are waking up to, the immortal inter-dimensional light being you are an eternal angelic being of light, a being of spirit for eternal you be.

All I wish is for all humans and all species in this universe to have inner peace, to project outer peace into the creation, to bring healing and balance in the Brahman, The Whole, The Creation. Blessings on your spiritual journey, blessings to all life in the creation of oneness, for oneness is all there be by love life lee.

OTHER BOOKS BY LOVELIFELEE

FRONT COVER

Expressions of life's journey, poems of
mystical experiences on my life's path
on planet Gaia & beyond.
Experiences of travelling around the world
and off world in the hyper-dimensional
matrix, some from in this universe & other
eternal realms. Experiences from
meditations, ancient spiritual practices,
plant medicines of Ayahuasca, Magic
Mushrooms, Salvia Divinorum, and
different forms of DMT
Dimethyltryptamine leaving my body
instantly travelling down wormholes
entering different dimensions of reality of
this holographical light university &
realities of the true nature outside time &
space in the eternal realm, poems of your
immortal light body & the hyper-
dimensional matrix the whole of the
brahman the creation Namaste lovelifelee

MER-KA-BA

BACK COVER

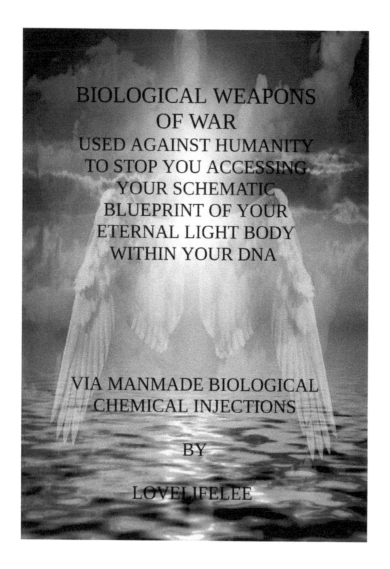

BIOLOGICAL WEAPONS
OF WAR
USED AGAINST HUMANITY
TO STOP YOU ACCESSING
YOUR SCHEMATIC
BLUEPRINT OF YOUR
ETERNAL LIGHT BODY
WITHIN YOUR DNA

VIA MANMADE BIOLOGICAL
CHEMICAL INJECTIONS

BY

LOVELIFELEE

FRONT COVER

This short book explains the truth behind the
psychological warfare conducted on the public
& biological weapon vaccines, the intention
behind them from the fallen angels cult to not
only to cull a large portion of humanity in their
eugenics program, but from the highest levels
of understanding, from the spiritual god
conscious perspective, from the awakened
human being to that of their eternal
immortality, on the understanding that the
vaccines will stop you accessing your light
body, via a schematic blueprint in your DNA,
also this book explains our cells and their
function and relationship to poisons.
This book also has an introduction to the DNA
blue print of instructions to grow a light body.

BACK COVER

OTHER BOOKS BY LOVELIFELEE

MILITARY GRADE WARFARE MICROWAVE WEAPON SYSTEMS

USED ON HUMANITY DESIGNED FOR NERVE BLOCK IN THE BIOLOGICAL BODY BY STARVING CELLS OF OXYGEN FALSELY UNDER THE GUISE OF TELECOMMUNICATION TECHNOLOGIES

TO STOP YOU ASCENDING & ACCESSING YOUR ETERNAL LIGHT BODY

BY

LOVE LIFE LEE

FRONT COVER

This short book exposes the military grade warfare microwave weapons systems in your homes 3G,4G and under the lying guise of telecommunications technologies 5G which are actually military microwave weapons designed to cause nerve block and starve the body of oxygen and can stop the heart, and manifesting our future reality.
Discussed also is understanding your cells their makeup and functions and their relationship to poisons especially microwave radiation poisoning.
An introduction to the DNA blueprint of instructions to grow a light body.

BACK COVER

OTHER BOOKS BY LOVELIFELEE

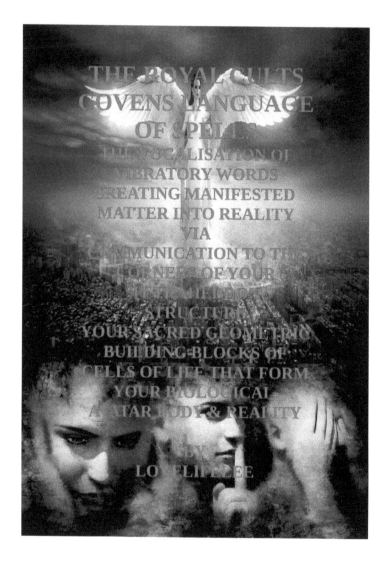

FRONT COVER

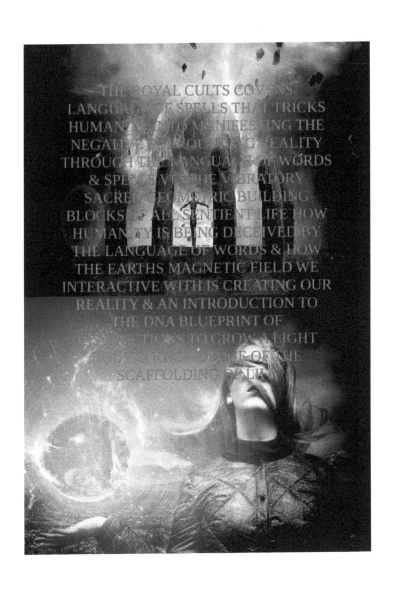

THE ROYAL CULTS COVEN'S LANGUAGE ARE SPELLS THAT TRICKS HUMANITY INTO MANIFESTING THE NEGATIVE AND CREATING REALITY THROUGH THE LANGUAGE OF WORDS & SPELLS VIA THE VIBRATORY SACRED GEOMETRIC BUILDING BLOCKS OF ALL SENTIENT LIFE HOW HUMANITY IS BEING DECEIVED BY THE LANGUAGE OF WORDS & HOW THE EARTHS MAGNETIC FIELD WE INTERACTIVE WITH IS CREATING OUR REALITY & AN INTRODUCTION TO THE DNA BLUEPRINT OF INSTRUCTIONS TO GROW A LIGHT BODY & KNOWLEDGE OF THE SCAFFOLDING OF ...

BACK COVER

OTHER BOOKS BY LOVELIFELEE

VEGAN RECIPES

PLANTS
ARE MEDICINE

PLANT FOOD FOR
YOUR CELLS THAT
FUEL & BUILD YOUR
SACRED GEOMETRIC
STRUCTURE

THE
SCAFFOLDING OF
LIFE

THATS
REGENERATING ON
A CONTINUUM

BY
LOVELIFELEE

FRONT COVER

THROUGH A VEGAN DIET GAIN ACCESS TO YOUR LIGHT BODY. VEGAN FOOD FUELS THE DODECAHEDRONS WITH AMINO ACIDS & THE TETRAHEDRONS WITH PROTEINS, THESE SACRED GEOMETRIC STRUCTURES ARE THE BUILDING BLOCKS OF, THE SCAFFOLDING OF LIFE YOUR BIOLOGICAL HUMAN AVATAR, THESE FOODS & VEGAN RECIPES WILL FUEL YOUR BODY & WITH OTHER SPIRITUAL PRACTICES & MEDITATION YOU WILL ACCESS YOUR ETERNAL LIGHT BODY.

DIET IS KEY

BY
LOVELIFELEE

BACK COVER

OTHER BOOKS BY LOVELIFELEE

FRONT COVER

LEARN ABOUT PLANT MEDICINES & MAKE YOUR OWN BE YOUR OWN DOCTOR [...] ARE AN ETERNAL LIGHT [...]

HEAL THE CELLS OF YOUR BIOLOGICAL HUMAN AVATAR BODY WITH [...] PLANT MEDICINES

PLANT MEDICINE & DIET IS KEY TO ACCESSING YOUR LUMINOUS ENERGY FIELD & RAISING YOUR BODY'S VIBRATION THUS RAISING YOUR CONSCIOUSNESS AND OPENING YOUR LIGHT BODY

LOVE LIFE LEE

BACK COVER

119

OTHER BOOKS BY LOVELIFELEE

FRONT COVER

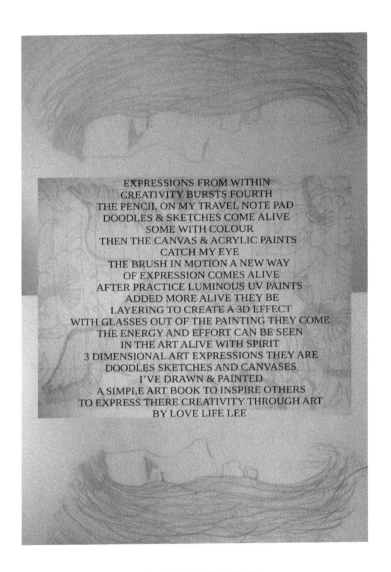

EXPRESSIONS FROM WITHIN
CREATIVITY BURSTS FOURTH
THE PENCIL ON MY TRAVEL NOTE PAD
DOODLES & SKETCHES COME ALIVE
SOME WITH COLOUR
THEN THE CANVAS & ACRYLIC PAINTS
CATCH MY EYE
THE BRUSH IN MOTION A NEW WAY
OF EXPRESSION COMES ALIVE
AFTER PRACTICE LUMINOUS UV PAINTS
ADDED MORE ALIVE THEY BE
LAYERING TO CREATE A 3D EFFECT
WITH GLASSES OUT OF THE PAINTING THEY COME
THE ENERGY AND EFFORT CAN BE SEEN
IN THE ART ALIVE WITH SPIRIT
3 DIMENSIONAL ART EXPRESSIONS THEY ARE
DOODLES SKETCHES AND CANVASES
I'VE DRAWN & PAINTED
A SIMPLE ART BOOK TO INSPIRE OTHERS
TO EXPRESS THERE CREATIVITY THROUGH ART
BY LOVE LIFE LEE

BACK COVER

PAGE INDEX OF BOOK

THE SINGLE PHOTON

The universe was created from a single photon, a particle of light, in which we human beings, and all beings are a fractal of that photon, but within our genetic make up is the whole photon. All light information of the universe, as well as what we see, outside and around us in the universe.

The universe is a three dimensional hologram of light, in all the colourful spectrums of light and made up of all sacred geometries patterns and shapes to create form from density, created by different vibrations, for us to experience in physical and non physical forms.

POEMS AND TRUTHS

OUR HOLOGRAPHIC UNIVERSE

THE PHOTON THE LIGHT PARTICLE

IN WHICH WE EXIST AND RESIDE UNTILL WE

EXPAND WITH LIGHT BRIGHTENING SHINING

BRIGHT IN OUR BODIES OF LIGHT ILLUMINATED

OUR RAINBOW BODIES FREE ANGELS WE BE

IMMORTAL INTERDIMENSIONAL LIGHT BEINGS OF

CONSCIOUS ENERGY

BY LOVE LIFE LEE

OTHER BOOKS BY LOVELIFELEE

DNA

DNA spirals, codes of all that be.

Life like you and me, and beyond all you can and can't see.

As well as density, high and low.

Vibrationally does the song of life evolve to be.

How inspirational all that can be.

DNA spirals, codes of light, so bright, in the colourful spectrum of light.

Sounds of a pure heart, manifest spirit of light, from the heart.

Conscious of all that be, of all that be. Conscious of all that be as one. Oneness is all that be.

A DEDICATION AND THANKS TO ALL THE PEOPLE
THAT ADVISED AND WHO INSPIRE ME ON THIS
BOOKS JOURNEY OF CREATION BLESSINGS TO YOU
ALL A.PWOLF THE WRITER AND DEAR FRIENDSHIP
THANKS FOR FIRST YOUR FRIENDSHIP AND HOURS
OF TIME SPENT BOUNCING IDEAS OFF EACH
OTHER OF SPIRITUAL MATTERS ANCIENT HISTORY
AND ALL POSSIBILITIES OF LIFE EXISTENCE IN ALL
DIMENSIONS AND FORMS, I DUCKING LOVE YOU
MADLY SOUL BROTHER BLESSED SPIRITS WE BE
YOU AND ME TRANSVERSING ENERGY
CONVERSING IN THE NOW CREATING WE BOTH BE
NAMASTE MY IMMORTAL SOUL BROTHER

THANKS TO MY SHAMANIC TEACHERS

IN THE AMAZON MAESTRO ENRIQUE

MAESTRA AYME MASTRO LOBO AND THE

SPIRIT OF THE PLANT MEDICINES

AYAHUASCA AND SO MANY OR PLANT

TEACHERS I'VE INGESTED.

THANK YOU MAURO THE AMAZON ARTIST

GRATITUDE YOU ARE INSPIRING BLESSINGS

THANK YOU TO SPIRITUAL RAINBOW

SISTER GERI MC-KELLAR FOR ALL THE

KNOWLEDGE TIME AND ENERGY YOU

HAVE GIVEN ME I APPRECIATE IT

ETERNALLY GRATITUDE AND BLESSINGS.

THANK YOU TO MY MUNAY-KI TEACHERS

IN THIS WORLD JULIANA FREEMAN AND

THOSE I VISIT OR CALL IN OPENING

PORTALS FROM THE IMMORTAL REALM

OUTSIDE OF LINER TIME AND SPACE THANK

YOU FOR HELPING ME GUIDING ME ON MY

JOURNEY OF SHEDDING THE PAST AND

TRANSCENDING TO OPEN MY LIGHT BODY

TO ASCEND AND QUANTUM LEAP TEN

THOUSAND YEARS INTO OUR BECOMING

THANKS TO MY FAMILY AND FRIENDS FOR

THE SUPPORT BLESSINGS TO ALL

THAT BE IN THE ONENESS OF CREATION

TRULY LOVE LIFE LEE NAMASTE